Random Thoughts of an Eternal Optimist

Corey Dee Williams

Introduction

Not every thought can apply to every situation, and just about everything has been said before in one way or another. I do not presume to be wise and all knowing... I just enjoy sharing thought provoking and random observations, without expectation. Each day it's up to us to take what we have been given, and create the mental outcome we choose. Learning is a growing experience... in fact everybody knows nothing, about something... as soon as we get rid of the notion of knowing, we can get back to the pursuit of learning. The solutions are found within.

Corey Dee Williams

Corey considers himself a man of a multitude of experiences, simple needs, and few wants. He was born in New York City and grew up in the borough of Manhattan in Harlem on St. Nicholas Avenue. A child of divorced parents, his father was an actor working hard to make a name for himself, who would eventually become a Hollywood icon. His mother was an independent woman, who would become one of the first ethnic models for Clairol, while working as an office manager for a Park Avenue dentist. Corey may be considered a so called "jack-of-all-trades" by many, but he is a multi-talented individual with numerous skills, and countless interesting stories to tell. He has done everything from modeling with his mother as a child, to song writing and music production. At age 12, he began Martial Arts training and credits this background as one of the influences for the optimistic and philosophical outlook he has today. Corey has been a lifelong fitness enthusiast, with over 30 years working as a premiere Fitness Lifestyle Coach. "When I began my career as a trainer, I quickly realized that helping people achieve their physical goal was most often more mental than physical." He began to adapt this approach with his clients to suite the personality of each individual, and created several fitness programs centered around the concept of body type training. Corey began to suffer from tachycardia in his 20's and eventually had a heart ablation at age 37. "Dealing with and recovering from tachycardia was one of the toughest times in my life." His eternal optimism comes from his ongoing desire to find a balance between reality and hope. "My optimism feeds off of my adversities… it doesn't originate from some misguided sense of reality, or exist due to a lack of difficulties in my life… quite the opposite! It is a choice! I feel the only purpose pessimism has, is to bring us to a more productive conclusion."

"The best time for optimism also happens to be the most difficult time."

1. It is not advantageous to regret choosing the road we have already traveled, though we can learn from it... we must face the road ahead.

2. Our weaknesses give us the opportunity to show strength... our strengths sometimes reveal weaknesses.

3. If we believe that an opportunity will never arrive... we will not be there to open the door when it knocks.

4. It may be difficult to see the other side of our situation... but the best time for optimism is usually the most difficult time.

5. We should never put our lives on hold, waiting for the chance, or the right moment to arise, passing up opportunities to enjoy it fully.

6. It becomes more difficult to enjoy the experience, if we are too focused on what is next.

7. People may not always understand our means of self expression... but that does not diminish its significance.

8. Know yourself... and no one will be able to convince you otherwise.

9. Getting to know oneself truly… is an exercise in the development of complete honesty, and awareness.

10. When we choose not to see
things as a struggle, the stress of
carrying that belief begins to
dissipate.

11. Our awareness… begins with self awareness… begins with genuine honesty.

12. Your level, is your own level... it is unnecessary to compare. Just grow.

13. Our heart may be in the right place, but it is of significance to align our heart with our actions.

14. So called advantages can become disadvantageous... so called disadvantages can become advantageous.

15. No need to declare ourselves to be anything… we just are, or are not.

16. Celebrity status, or notoriety, does not make someone extraordinary, the amount of humility that one possesses along with it does.

17. In this time of social self indulgence... lets take a moment to shift attention to others, and see what happens...

18. There is never any need to defend our thoughts, or emotions. The correct interpretation is our own.

19. Never use your ego as a cornerstone to build the foundation of your humility on.

20. Success and failure are only arbitrary results... it is up to us what we choose to do with them.

21. We may receive more of what we desire, when we take time to appreciate what we already have.

22. Let's learn to appreciate the imperfections today, and see what happens...

23. No problem ever deserves as much attention as the solution.

24. Criticism is 99% useless and 1% helpful... unless solicited.

25. Never let anyone talk you out of accomplishing something... especially yourself.

26. Everyone wants to be sexy...
but don't forget to put your soul
before your sex appeal.

27. The feeling of regret, only connects us to a past that can never be altered... tomorrow, today will be yesterday... therefore, right now matters the most.

28. Success is like air, we can breathe it in, but eventually we need to exhale.

29. Our time may be valuable... but the time we give is invaluable, and should never be taken for granted.

30. Our status is irrelevant... the true indicator of who we are, is our treatment of others. The genuine will remain genuine.

31. Never allow what you seek,
to blind you from seeing what is
right in front of you.

32. We are truly capable of making our own luck... through our choices.

33. Never allow someone else's negativity to become your own. Let them keep it.

34. Let's focus on our resolve today... reduce the significance of appreciation... and see what happens...

35. True optimism is having absolutely no reason to be optimistic... then discovering we don't need one!

36. Let's not forget, to
occasionally look beyond our
own little world... and lend our
consideration to others.

37. The most valuable actions are driven by selflessness.

38. Let's smile at the frowns today... and see what happens...

39. Give more attention to the opportunity in front of you, and worry less about the one that is not... then see what happens...

40. If we recognize all that the moment has to offer, including the negative... we may better understand where it leads us.

41. The more familiar we become with ourselves… the closer we get to discovering fulfillment.

42. Perfection is an illusion, which can also be perceived within imperfection.

43. Once we strip away the need to be something, or someone... we are free to be what we truly are.

44. Great rewards seldom come without tribulation. Persevere.

45. Each day it's up to us, to use circumstances to create an outcome we choose.

46. Real communication, sometimes requires reaching beyond our own agenda.

47. Keep your standards high…
and give everyone the opportunity to rise up to them.

48. Individually, like a thumbprint... we each have something completely unique to offer. Be you!

49. Good times can be found wherever the heart is, we create them.

50. Some things may happen for a reason, some for no good reason at all... but what we do with the experiences is our choice.

51. Opportunities can be found hiding within difficulties.

52. Genuine love comes in a multitude of expressions… there is nothing to fear in simply acknowledging its presence.

53. When we move past negativity of others, we take away its power.

54. The main ingredient for the recipe of a great day today, is optimism.

55. Let's resist the urge to be confrontational today... and see what happens...

56. The journey often has as much to offer as the destination... appreciate the road that brings you along.

57. Let's acknowledge our own worth... and also let someone know how much we appreciate them today.

58. Let's take all criticism as opinion, and use it to our advantage today... then see what happens...

59. Our professed love for someone, does not afford us the right to be disrespectful or inconsiderate.

60. We can live with our eyes wide open, yet sometimes we only see what we want to see.

61. Success and failure are simply experiences... that bring us to the next opportunity.

62. Let's let go of the problem today... give the solution undivided attention... and see what happens...

63. Today… Let's avoid allowing anyone else's attitude to affect ours… and see what happens…

64. Never get discouraged! Many things are definite... but very few are absolute.

65. When we choose to define others, we see them through eyes that include the imperfections of our own vision.

66. Our inner happiness and contentment is a measure of our gratitude.

67. There are no setbacks, only experiences... time moves in one direction... Forward!

68. The road behind us, brought us to this destination... but the road we choose now is the most significant.

69. Let's encourage, motivate… and tell ourselves exactly what we need to hear today!

70. We should never allow the fear of uncertainty to hinder our progress.

71. If we spend less time worrying about being impressive, we have more time to simply be ourselves.

72. Today… let's not allow the frenetic energy of others, to become our own.

73. Stand firm, but be flexible… Confident, but humble.

74. Let's avoid the need to become defensive today... and see what happens...

75. Opinions can sometimes be helpful, but they may also be very loosely based on our own truth, or reality.

76. We should always remember to give our friends the same consideration as our successes.

77. We can spend our time choosing to see the flaws in all things, or use our time to appreciate the beauty.

78. Each of us may see things differently... no need to correct others into submission. Communicate by example.

79. Today... let go of anger... let go of animosity... let go of resentment... and see what happens...

80. The greatest limitation… is having a limited perception of what is possible.

81. There is a current of change flowing through our lives... we can swim against it, or learn to swim with it.

82. Let's leave the past behind... the future ahead... and give this moment our undivided attention.

83. Our word is a priceless commodity... it can be given, but should always be kept.

84. State your experiences in a way that describes them in a positive manner... and see what happens...

85. Today… let go of aggravation, let go of frustration, let go of blame … and see what happens…

86. To effect significant change… We need to spend more time perpetuating what is right with the world, and less promoting what is wrong with it.

87. It matters very little how others choose to define us... or even how we choose to define ourselves. We can only be exactly what we truly are.

88. Believing we are here to teach everyone can be more limiting than learning from the experience.

89. We can spend our time waiting for the right moment to be happy, or we can create one.

90. Never let a problem become a distraction from the solution at hand.

91. Our treatment of others begins with self awareness... be kind and considerate to yourself and to others.

92. Even seemingly negative aspects of change can help shape a more desirable existence.

93. When we let go of the need for approval, we are free to be who we truly are.

94. It isn't the cards we've been dealt... it's how we play the hand, that matters most.

95. Most often... when we let go of one thing, we gain something else.

96. Recognize the natural occurrences, that may lead us in a new direction... and allow them to occur.

97. We should revel in our own abilities... but also celebrate and support the talents of our friends.

98. True confidence is letting go of the outcome.

99. When we close our mind to possibilities, we shut the door on opportunities.

100. The most valuable lesson… is the "mistake" we can recognize as being a lesson.

101. Whether we feel we are stepping backwards, or forwards… it's all a part of the same dance.

102. Sometimes... our time is actually not the time, and we need to allow things to happen on their own time... right on time.

103. The best way to avoid
having any so called
"disadvantages" take control of
our life, is to deny them any
purpose.

104. Expect nothing... be prepared for anything, and disappointments will be few.

105. Sometimes we wait for our circumstances to change, without realizing the circumstances may be there to change us.

106. The real difficulty is not in accomplishing something... it is overcoming the limiting belief that it will be too difficult.

107. The value of our effort is not defined by validation, or the lack of... but rather our own feeling of accomplishment.

108. Getting to TRULY know oneself is an exercise in complete honesty... it is independence from the judgement of others.

109. If we focus too intently on achieving the end result, we may become distracted from actually doing what is necessary to achieve it.

110. Opinions are sometimes like false truths... we can allow them to discourage us, or use them to motivate us.

111. Happiness is a personal choice... nobody can define it for us based on their own ideals. Find gratitude, and happiness will follow you.

112. We should never lose sight of the fact... negatives often become positives, and positives may become negatives. We only need to concern ourselves with our reaction, and interaction. It can all be beneficial in some way.

113. Often, attempting to change someone's view by arguing, is like trying to persuade a hippo to become a giraffe. Examples lead.

114. If we have not learned to find internal joy where we are, we may never experience happiness where we are going.

115. We can focus on everything that is wrong with the conditions, or choose to take advantage of everything that is right with them.

Corey Dee's Seven Random Symbols

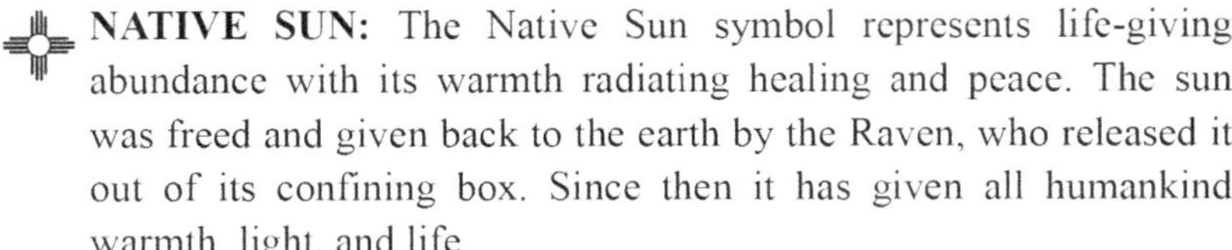

NATIVE SUN: The Native Sun symbol represents life-giving abundance with its warmth radiating healing and peace. The sun was freed and given back to the earth by the Raven, who released it out of its confining box. Since then it has given all humankind warmth, light, and life.

BASS: A Bass clef placing F below middle C on the second-highest line of the staff.

LOTUS: The Lotus Flower is regarded in many different cultures, especially in Eastern religions, as a symbol of purity, enlightenment, self-regeneration and rebirth. Its characteristics are a perfect analogy for the human condition: even when its roots are in the dirtiest waters, the Lotus produces the most beautiful flower.

EAGLE: The Native Americans were tribes of deeply spiritual people.Since we know the eagles fly the highest, the Native Americans believe that they are the closest creatures to the Creator. The eagle symbol meaning in their culture is of strength, wisdom, and courage.

HEART WINGS: A Heart with Wings is not only used to symbolize free spirit, but also freedom from certain things like addiction or bad habits.Sometimes, a heart with wings is used to symbolize freedom in love, love for freedom to maintain one's will and individuality.

LEO: Leo is represented by the lion, and these spirited fire signs are the kings and queens of the celestial jungle. They're delighted to embrace their royal status: vivacious, theatrical, and passionate, **Leos** love to bask in the spotlight and celebrate themselves.

HEALER'S HAND: The Healer's Hand, also known as the Shaman's Hand, is an ancient symbol of healing and protection. The image consists of a hand with a spiral palm and it is believed to have come from the Native American solar hieroglyphs that have been found in a number of places in the south-western part of the United States.

SUMMARY / EXPRESS YOUR OWN RANDOM THOUGHTS

SUMMARY / EXPRESS YOUR OWN RANDOM THOUGHTS